C000254650

Do Not Let Your Hearts Be Troubled

Thoughts on Ministry to the Terminally Ill

Edward Daly

First published 2004 by
Veritas Publications
7/8 Lower Abbey Street
Dublin 1
Ireland
Email publications@veritas.ie
Website www.veritas.ie

ISBN 1 85390 825 8

10 9 8 7 6 5 4 3 2

Acknowledgements
Texts of Scripture readings are taken from
The Jerusalem Bible, copyright © 1966
by Darton, Longman and Todd Ltd.

Psalm text from *The Psalms: A New Translation*
© The Grail (England) 1963.

Printed in the Republic of Ireland
by Paceprint Dublin

Veritas books are printed on paper made from the
wood pulp of managed forests. For every tree felled,
at least one tree is planted, thereby renewing natural
resources.

'People should be able to hold someone's hand when they are dying, but a human hand must never be the cause of their death'

Cardinal Franz König of Vienna

Contents

Foreword

IT IS MY EXPERIENCE that most people do not fear death, but they are extremely scared of dying. It is not so much death as the process of getting there that is the greater cause of concern. The mechanics of dying, the last months and weeks before death, and the dread of parting from loved ones can be extremely difficult and frustrating for terminally ill patients and for their nearest and dearest.

For the last ten years, since 1994, my ministry has been dedicated to accompanying people and their families on that journey, the last few weeks and months of their pilgrimage through this life. I have served as chaplain to the In-Patient Unit in the Foyle Hospice in Derry. I consider it a great privilege to be involved in this ministry. It has been and continues to be a wonderful experience. It is a situation in which one is forever learning, forever being challenged – challenged emotionally and physically, and frequently challenged spiritually. It is wonderful to have the luxury of time – all the time in the world to spend with people, with patients and their families – a luxury that few serving priests or bishops have the opportunity to experience. These have been the most fulfilling years of my entire priesthood. Ministry takes on a whole new dimension in a hospice situation.

Prior to engaging in this ministry, I had served as a curate in two parishes in the Derry Diocese for sixteen years, then spent seven or eight months working in broadcasting in RTÉ in Dublin, and subsequently served for almost twenty years as Bishop of Derry. I had my first personal confrontation with cancer in 1977 when I had my left kidney removed because of a malignant tumour. In February 1993 I had a moderate right-sided stroke. My right arm and leg, some fingers on my right hand, my speech and swallowing were inhibited to the extent that six months later my doctor advised me to submit my retirement as bishop. The Holy Father kindly accepted my resignation in late 1993. With intensive physiotherapy and speech therapy and endless hours of physical and speech exercise before the mirror at home, I have been graced with a wonderful recovery from the stroke. Apart from intense fatigue in the latter part of the day and a slight problem with my right leg on steps and stairs, I am not aware of any residual problems from that experience. In 1999, the cancer returned and I had a tumour removed from my lung. I have found that my experience of serious illness and cancer was of some assistance to me in ministering to those undergoing similar experiences, albeit more acute. The accumulated and varied experiences garnered over thirty-seven years of active priesthood and life prepared me for my new ministry. However, I have to admit that I embarked upon it with a certain amount of apprehension.

I have enormous respect and admiration for Dr Tom McGinley. His magnificent vision and courage brought the Foyle Hospice into being. He has been Medical Director since its foundation. I am deeply indebted to him for his valuable assistance with this book. The doctors and nurses who have served in the In Patient Unit over the past ten years, Home Care and Day Care nurses have all been an inspiration to me. The other members of staff and volunteers, my colleagues as chaplains, the families and friends of patients, past and present, the Choir and the Liturgy Group, have all contributed, unwittingly or not, to this book. Like them, I am pleased and honoured to be part of the Foyle Hospice family.

This little book is essentially a reflection on my experience as a chaplain in the Foyle Hospice. I hope that it might be of some small help or comfort to those ministering in similar situations or to those experiencing terminal illness or their families.

CHAPTER 1

The Hospice

THE IRISH SISTERS of Charity pioneered the hospice movement. Having founded Our Lady's Hospice in Dublin, they established St Joseph's Hospice in Hackney in the East End of London in 1905. Hospice care, however, took on a new dimension in 1966 with the opening of St Christopher's Hospice in London. This was to be the start of the modern hospice movement. Dame Cecily Saunders, who had studied pain and symptom control in great detail at St Joseph's Hospice after she qualified as a doctor, was the inspiration behind St Christopher's and became the first medical director there. The caring art of medicine was coupled with the sensitive application of the scientific method. There was also a major commitment to teaching the newfound knowledge and expertise. Dame Cecily Saunders' contribution to the modern hospice movement has been immense and the number of hospices, nationally and internationally, has increased rapidly since the early seventies.

As hospices and specialist care skills developed in Ireland and the UK, many patients who were admitted to hospices with distressing pain and other symptoms were able to be discharged back to their own homes. This precipitated the need for hospices to develop their own Home Care teams. These specialised nurses started to visit patients in their own homes, advising and liaising with general practitioners and district nurses. Gradually they were also invited into hospitals to advise on symptom control for patients with advanced cancer. With 'hospice type' care being disseminated into hospitals and the general community it became widely accepted that this care was indeed a concept of care that would not be confined to specific places or institutions. The focus of hospice-type care was broad and holistic. The general term 'palliative care' became adopted.

Palliative care has become synonymous with hospice care. Palliative care is the active total care of patients and their families by a multi-professional team when the patient's disease is no longer responsive to curative treatment. The term palliative care comes from the Latin word 'palliatus' meaning 'cloaked' or 'protected'. In the early years of the development of hospice, 'terminal care' was the term most frequently used. More recently palliative care has been applied and palliative medicine has now been included in the list of recognised specialities.

There is a distinction between palliative care and terminal care. Many patients are now referred for symptom control and advice in the early stages of their cancer journey. It would be totally wrong to say that they are terminal as some will live for many years and many others may die from some other condition not related to their cancer. Palliative care is concerned with enabling and facilitating; it focuses on what can be achieved and what is still possible. It is deeply respectful of the unique worth and value of each person regardless of their disease state or functional status. Care of the family and those who matter to the patient is an integral part of the overall package of care. Terminal care should be restricted to describing the stage of a patient's illness when it becomes clear that death is imminent and most likely to occur within days or weeks. In those circumstances, terminal care becomes an integral part of palliative care and not a separate entity.

Dr Tom McGinley is the founder and first Medical Director of the Foyle Hospice. The Foyle Hospice had been his ambition and dream for many years. He was the driving force behind it. He had been a much respected General Practitioner in Derry City for more than thirty years and identified a need for a hospice in the area. I shared this vision; many years of sick visitation had persuaded me of the need for a hospice. With local councils, community and church leaders in the North West, I supported Dr McGinley in pursuing this objective since it was first mooted in 1983. Two Home Care Nurses were appointed and began their work in 1985. That work continues in patients' homes throughout the area and is co-ordinated, controlled and administered from the hospice. The detailed knowledge of hospice care and training required for community was acquired in St Joseph's Hospice in London and St Mary's Hospice in Birmingham.

The In-Patient Unit of the Foyle Hospice was opened on Thursday 20 June 1991, a gloriously sunny day. It was formally opened by two young girls, Claire and Emma, one from the Catholic community, the other from the Protestant community. Both had lost their mothers to cancer and our Home Care Nurses had helped to look after both women. The In-Patient Unit has twelve beds, as well as four family rooms and an educational unit. The nearby Day Care Unit was opened early in May 2002. On our staff we have a medical director, matron, four home care nurses, twenty staff nurses, four administration staff, seven fundraising staff and a large number of volunteers.

The nearby Foyle Bridge was adopted as the symbol or logo of the hospice – because the hospice is truly a bridge between both sides of the city, between both communities in the North West and is also, for many, the bridge between this life and the next.

The Foyle Hospice serves the geographical area of Derry City, the surrounding areas in Counties Derry and Tyrone and the Inishowen Peninsula in Donegal. The hospice is a Charitable Trust generously supported by all sections of the community in the North West on both sides of the border. The community met the entire capital expenditure of both buildings amounting to approximately £3 million. The community continues to contribute 70 per cent of the running costs (£1.5 per annum). Since it opened, the Foyle Hospice has constantly had 85-100 per cent bed occupancy.

As compared with hospitals, hospices are relatively small units. I have come to look upon the Foyle Hospice more as a family, as a group of people rather than a place. At the very centre and core of that family are the patients, then there are the patients' families, their nearest and dearest, the medical and nursing staff of the hospice, the chaplains and other services, the volunteers who give of their time and service on a voluntary basis, the families of former patients, and the people of the North West who support the hospice in so many different ways. Each element is supportive of every other element in the hospice family. There is a wonderful unity of purpose, a sense of togetherness. It is, to my mind, a perfect example of Christianity in action.

When I became part of the Hospice Caring Team, it was my first experience of being part of a team that was predominantly female. For most of my life, as priest and bishop, I had worked in an environment where my colleagues were predominantly male. It was part of the culture shock that I experienced when I began work in the hospice. I have always held nurses in very high esteem, but, during the last ten years, I have come to have an even deeper appreciation of their qualities and of their work. With the exception of two excellent male nurses, all the members of the nursing staff in the Foyle Hospice over the past ten years have been female. They are great colleagues, wonderfully skilled, and people who are most caring. Hospice nursing requires special personal and professional skills. The work can be very demanding emotionally and physically. I have witnessed, at first hand, the powerful feminine dimension of care. Nurses are most affirming colleagues and they can be critical where and when criticism is required. Many of them have a wonderful sense of humour and, as a result, the hospice is a very happy working environment. I have always felt very comfortable working there.

Our patients come from all over the North West, from all denominations and classes and from both sides of the Irish border. They are rather like Christy Moore's memorable description of the people who attended Lisdoonvarna! They have ranged in age from children to people in their eighties. Most of the patients are suffering from advanced stages of various forms of cancer. We have also cared for people with other life threatening diseases such as motor neurone disease and advanced renal and respiratory disease.

When I first came to Derry in 1962, I remember being called by a family to speak to their mother. She was an elderly woman and the family asked me to try to persuade her to go to hospital for necessary treatment. Altnagelvin Hospital had just been opened in Derry. I asked her why she did not want to go. She pointed out the obituary column in the local newspaper, 'Do you see how many people die there in that new hospital?' she exclaimed with great indignation. Eventually, after some gentle persuasion and with considerable reluctance, she agreed to go.

Many of us are similarly reluctant to go to hospital, reluctant even to go to a doctor. We feel a pain or discomfort or a lump; we hope it will go away; it doesn't; then we fear that it is something sinister; then we don't go to the doctor in case we find out that it may be serious! Such a reaction is understandable, but it is irresponsible.

For similar reasons, some people, too, are very reluctant to be admitted to a hospice. The decision to seek admission to the hospice is very difficult for many patients and their families. It is a huge decision. The hospice here in the North West, as already mentioned, is a relatively new form of institution. In the minds of some, there is still something akin to a stigma attached to it. They believe that it is the end of the road. Many families of patients, too, share in this reluctance. They have a feeling that if they admit their loved one to a hospice, it somehow implies that they are either unwilling or unable to nurse the patient at home. Many families of patients have told me that they felt a profound sense of guilt about agreeing to admit a family member as a patient. Such guilt or fears are understandable but they are misplaced and unjustified. Few families have the requisite skills and resources to treat a terminally ill patient as well as he or she can be cared for in a hospice. This becomes clear to such people as soon as they experience a hospice environment. Once people are admitted as patients to the hospice, the patients and their families very quickly adapt to their new surroundings; they settle down, they feel secure and comfortable; their initial fears or worries evaporate. They receive a quality of care that could not be delivered at home, even with best goodwill in the world. In some cases, it may well be the end of the road, the last stop on a long journey. But, in some other cases, patients are admitted for pain control and other types of palliative care and are subsequently able to return home to their families, feeling much better and enjoying an improved quality of life.

There is no justification for any feelings of guilt about admitting a family member to a hospice. I believe that such a decision is in the best interests of the patient.

The patients arriving with us are often tired and exhausted. Since first receiving their diagnosis, many of them have spent weeks or months going through a series of tests and scans, perhaps undergoing major surgery on one or more occasions; they may have experienced chemotherapy or radiotherapy – they have been patients in their local hospital, and been to hospitals in Belfast or Dublin, such as Belvoir or St Luke's. They have undergone repeated lengthy road journeys for treatment or hospital appointments when they felt unwell. They have tried to rationalise what has been happening to them. In some cases, there has been substantial hair loss and their physical appearance has radically changed. Their self-esteem has suffered. Many of them are frightened and bewildered. Their life and the lives of their families have been turned upside down. Future plans have been put on hold. The words of Jesus in St Matthew's Gospel often come to mind,

> Come to me, all you who labour and are overburdened, and I will give you rest. Shoulder my yoke and learn from me, for I am gentle and humble in heart, and you will find rest for your souls.
> (Matthew 11:28-30).

That quotation is particularly apt for a hospice or hospice care. People who experience a long battle with cancer are certainly overburdened.

I feel that the role of a hospice is to share the patient's burden in some way, to assist the patient in carrying his or her burden. The medical staff will do everything possible to make the patient comfortable, to control pain and nausea, to deal with the patient's physical pain. But often there are other forms of pain there as well. There is loneliness, fear, disbelief that this could happen, worries about family and work and business, worries about how the people left behind are going to cope – emotional pain, spiritual pain, pain of the soul. There is also questioning about how 'a loving God' can allow something like this to intervene so destructively in his or her life. These emotions are often shared by members of the patient's family. So the ministry to the patient inevitably includes ministry to the patient's family. I perceive hospice chaplaincy as a ministry of accompaniment of the patient and the patient's family – travelling the journey with them.

The Foyle Hospice environment is not like that of a hospital. It is perhaps more like that of a hotel! It is a single storey complex that fits admirably into the environment. There is a large foyer and reception area furnished with comfortable settees, armchairs and handsome carpets. There is an admirable collection of paintings on the walls throughout the building. All of the patients' beds and rooms look out on flowers and shrubs, with a large field beyond, where horses graze. In the near distance is the aforementioned magnificent and graceful Foyle Bridge spanning the River Foyle, and beyond that is the ever-growing Waterside area and in the far distance to the south-east, the Sperrin Mountains loom into view. There is woodland nearby, too, and in the early morning, if you are lucky, you will see a fox or badger hunting or prowling and there are the ubiquitous rabbits scampering around – all of this offers an interesting and ever-changing panorama that all our patients enjoy. It is relaxing and therapeutic. It is difficult to realise that it is located on the edge of a busy city. It is more like a rural setting.

The site was formerly the property of the Orange Order from which the hospice purchased it. It was purchased by the Order in 1953 and between that time and 1969 they held their Twelfth of July rally there every fourth year. The site extends right to the river bank close to where the boom was located across the River Foyle during the Siege of Derry in 1689. St Colmcille sailed down that same river in his currach on his way to found his monastery in Iona more than a thousand years earlier in the sixth century. Hundreds of thousands of emigrants from the northwest passed there on sailing ships on their way to the New World in the nineteenth century. The river was Derry's commercial lifeline for centuries. There is certainly no shortage of conversational topics when looking out on that site. Some years ago, we had a patient whose husband was a ship's pilot on the River Foyle. When he was piloting oil tankers up the river to the mooring further upstream, he always sounded the ship's horn when he was passing the hospice to let his wife know that he was thinking of her.

The first twenty-four hours after admission to a hospice are very important. Patients are given lots of time to settle into their new and foreign environment. A doctor and senior staff nurse will meet the patient and their family and acquire all the information that they require or seek further elaboration on the information sent by the patient's hospital or GP. If the patient is registered as a Catholic, I may pay a brief visit shortly after their admission just to introduce myself and advise the patient of my availability at all times. I am in a fortunate position, because most patients know me already. I have spent the last forty-two years in Derry City, and served as bishop here for twenty years; as a result, a lot of people in the North West know me. I find that I have met a large number of the patients before in various circumstances, especially during the celebration of Confirmation of either themselves or their children or grandchildren. This is a considerable advantage and makes the task of introduction less difficult than it might be.

Chapter 2

The Patient

THE MORNING VISIT to patients in the hospice is always one the highlights of my day. If the patient is able to talk or communicate, we usually chat about various things – the news, the weather, sport, family – about how the night went, how they slept. Some patients are unable to carry on a conversation, because of breathlessness, because they have had a tracheotomy or for other reasons. If the patient is unable to converse, I try to talk to them. With the help of their families, I try to ascertain their interests, and take the opportunity to focus on some of these topics. Then we gradually ease our way into prayer and perhaps talk about the saint whose feast day it is, or the liturgical season – Lent, or Easter or Pentecost or Christmas. I may read a piece of scripture and reflect on it. I then give them Holy Communion, share the Eucharist with them. If members of the family are present, as is frequently the case, they may share in the Eucharist, if they so wish. We then observe a period of silence, reflection and prayer. The visit is unhurried.

In the course of my hospice ministry, I meet people who have been devout and committed churchgoers and who have endeavoured to live their faith throughout their lives. I meet people who have not set foot in a church or received the sacraments for years. I do not meet many people who are apathetic – I suppose there is not much room for apathy in a hospice. I have met a few people who were angry and resentful at the Church, because of something that was said or done by a priest or bishop in years gone by. Living in a divided and troubled society such as ours where harsh things were said and done – or not done – in very difficult times, it was easy to be hurt. There are people who are angry with God, irritated and frustrated that they are so ill and that their lives and the lives of their families have been so disrupted. Despite their anger and hurt, all these people were kind and welcoming to me. When I volunteered to serve as chaplain, I may have thought that I would be ministering to the patients; I had not anticipated that, in some cases, the patients would be ministering to me!

There is a powerful honesty within a hospice situation. It is not a place for making a big impression. The discussions with patients are usually very open and revealing. They say what they feel, what they believe. They give expression to their emotions and frustrations. There is no point in hiding anything at that stage of life. Nothing is held back. Such people deserve an equally open and revealing response. Again and again, I have been forced to ask myself very difficult questions. Most patients want someone to listen to what they have to say. They do not necessarily expect answers to their questions. But they want their questions to be heard. Listening to patients, in many situations, is more important than speaking to them.

Sometimes a member of a family will come shortly after a patient is admitted and say 'My father doesn't know that he is seriously ill. He is not aware of the diagnosis or prognosis, he doesn't know that he is terminally ill. So please be careful and do not mention that for the time being.' On a subsequent visit to the patient concerned, he will say 'I am not going to get better. I am aware of that, but I don't think my family are fully aware of that. I'm not sure how they would cope with it!' Both parties are going on tip-toe around the issue, walking on eggshells. Both parties are aware of the situation, but they find themselves unable to discuss it and believe that the other party is unaware. There is a heightened consciousness of terminal illness nowadays. Most people have some familiarity with the choreography, for want of a better word; they can read the signs and are familiar with the procedures and symptoms associated with it. People are much better informed than in the past. In most situations, both the patient and the family are aware of the possible outcome. But, in some instances, they find themselves unable to communicate with one another about it. They will discuss anything but 'the elephant in the corner'. Such denial puts enormous stress on both the patient and the family members. The best possible scenario in a hospice setting is that both the patient and the family know the full story and, with or without support, are able to talk to one another about it. There is so much to be gained from such a situation; it is so beneficial to all concerned.

In the situation where there is difficulty in communication of this nature, those of us who serve in the hospice have a role. We respect the individual's right to maintain his or her position, but, at the same time, we encourage each party to talk to the other. We may serve as intermediaries in such situations. We may let one party know that the other is aware of the situation, if permission is granted to do so. As mentioned already, it is so much better when each party is aware that the other party knows the reality of the situation. This may seem to relatives to be an insurmountable obstacle, but it can usually be overcome with gentle sensitivity on all sides.

During my morning visits, I pick up on various matters. The patient may be afraid. He or she may be troubled; there may be family or other problems that they wish to discuss. If I perceive that a patient wants to talk to me in further detail and at greater length, I will call back later at a quiet time of the day and make myself available for as long as is necessary. Sometimes patients wish to talk; sometimes they do not want to talk or be disturbed. The wishes of the patient are always respected.

When patients are very ill, I would try to call with them a few times during the day.

I liaise closely with the medical staff, with the doctors and nurses. They may bring issues to my attention. Confidentiality, however, is very much respected on both sides. The matron or senior staff nurse advises me on new admissions, discharges and transfers to hospitals and so on. There is a very high ratio of staff to patient. This ensures that all the patients receive very generous attention from the staff. The members of the nursing staff in the Foyle Hospice are of a very high calibre. The work, at times, can be taxing physically and emotionally. When you share a patient's suffering, travel the journey with a patient and a patient's family, you become keenly aware of your own inadequacies and of your own blessings. You become even more grateful and appreciative of the blessing of good health and the blessing of good friends. Such an experience offers a new perspective on life – and on death.

CHAPTER 3

Prayer and Sacraments

THE MOST POWERFUL and important comforts that I have to offer to the patients in the hospice are the sacraments and the word of God. During recent years, I have come to a new appreciation of the immense value of the sacraments and sacramentals as a source of grace and human comfort. I have also come to a deeper appreciation of the power and beauty and relevance of God's word. Here one has the opportunity to administer the sacraments and to remain in close daily contact with the recipient for a considerable period after the sacrament is administered. It is a pastoral opportunity seldom experienced outside the hospice situation. The tactile sacraments such as the Anointing of the Sick can be powerful, physically as well as spiritually. Administering a sacrament can be an occasion that is prayerful and comforting and affirming for both recipient and minister. I administer the Sacrament of Anointing to all our Catholic patients once every month. I endeavour to explain the meaning of the sacrament to them

– and frequently read the passage from chapter five of the Letter of St James (5:14-15):

> If one of you is ill, he should send for the elders of the church, and they must anoint him with oil in the name of the Lord and pray over him. The prayer of faith will save the sick man and the Lord will raise him up again; and if he has committed any sins, he will be forgiven.

Before the anointing, we usually celebrate the Sacrament of Reconciliation – we make our peace with God and all our brothers and sisters. We take plenty of time. There is never any hurry. We may read a passage from the Gospels about Jesus ministering to the sick. We may reflect about that. I explain the origin of the Oil of the Sick, that it was blessed in the cathedral on the previous Holy Thursday by the bishop in the presence of priests and people. Then some short prayers are recited, and I impose my hands on the head of the patient who is to be anointed and subsequently anoint the forehead saying 'Through this holy anointing, may the Lord in his love and mercy help you with the grace of the Holy Spirit'. The palms of the hands are then anointed saying 'May the Lord who frees you from sin save you and raise you up'. In some cases, other parts of the body that are the source or location of considerable pain or discomfort are anointed. I like to use liberal amounts of the oil. Then there is a period of prayer – there are beautiful prayers in the *Pastoral Care of the Sick*.[1] I read one or more of these prayers and then together we recite the Lord's Prayer and finally I give the Eucharist, Holy Communion, to the patient.

This is a beautiful liturgy. I came to a new appreciation of it when I received it on several occasions during my own experiences of illness. I had a wonderful sense of peace after being anointed, an immensely pleasurable and calming peace. In my early years of priesthood, the Anointing of the Sick was perceived by many as 'The Last Rites' or the 'The Last Sacraments' and was only administered in the event of imminent death. In the post-Vatican II liturgical dispensation, it is understood in a different way and it is offered to people who have a serious or severe illness or before surgery. This, I believe, is a more accurate and generous response to the exhortation of St James in his letter.

It is interesting that some of the modern alternative therapies, such as aromatherapy, use the anointing with oil as part of their treatment. In our Day Centre in the Hospice, some of these alternative therapies are made available. The anointing with oil allied with prayer in a sacramental context is extraordinarily powerful.

In the aforementioned book, *Pastoral Care of the Sick*, there are many scriptural readings and suggestions for prayer. Some patients like to hear

---

1 *Pastoral Care of the Sick – Rites of Anointing and Viaticum* Dublin: Veritas Publications (It is the ritual used by most priests in Ireland when attending the sick)

passages from scripture read to them and I enjoy reading them in such circumstances. I bring my Bible or my breviary or other books containing scripture passages and we read them and chat about them, apply them to ourselves and reflect on them and pray about them together. Reading scripture aloud on a one-to-one basis can lead into some amazing journeys. We begin with prayer and can end anywhere. One of my favourite passages for reading to patients is the beautiful passage from John chapter 14, verses 1-23. Jesus is talking to his disciples at the Last Supper. He is aware that they are apprehensive about what lies ahead during that night and the following day. He urges them with the words 'do not let your hearts be troubled'. He asks them to 'Trust in God still and trust in me'. He points out that he is 'the Way, the Truth and the Life'. It is a wonderfully comforting passage. Patients ask that it be read again and again and quite a few subsequently request their families to have it read as the Gospel reading at their funeral Mass. All those chapters in St John's Gospel, chapters fourteen to seventeen, are full of inspirational passages – passages written to encourage and reassure and reaffirm people and have particular impact and significance in a hospice setting.

I also like to read the words of hymns to patients – one of my favourite hymns and prayers being Cardinal Newman's 'Lead Kindly Light':

> Lead, kindly Light, amid the encircling gloom,

Lead thou me on;
The night is dark, and I am far from home,
Lead thou me on.
Keep thou my feet; I do not ask to see
The distant scene; one step enough for me.

I was not ever thus, nor prayed that thou
Shouldst lead me on;
I loved to choose and see my path; but now
Lead thou me on.
I loved the garish day, and, spite of fears,
Pride ruled my will: remember not past
years.

So long thy power hath blest me, sure it still
Will lead me on
O'er moor and fen, o'er crag and torrent, till
The night is gone,
And with the morn, those Angel faces smile,
Which I have loved long since, and lost
awhile.

The words of this prayer and hymn are beautiful
and uplifting and particularly comforting. It is a
great act of faith and confidence in God, an act of
acceptance of God's will. 'I loved to choose and see
my path; but now lead thou me on'. It is a prayer of
abandonment into God's hands. When it is slowly
read and prayed aloud it has great power and
significance.

But people's favourite prayers are usually the
simple prayers that they learned in childhood.

Some of them have prayed them all their lives. Others have not bothered much about them. But most people of my age remember them. The Our Father and Hail Mary, the Memorare, Salve Regina, Prayer to the Angel Guardian and Prayer for a Happy Death are the favourite prayers of most patients. Many people have, during their lives, adopted certain devotions. Some people, men as well as women, have a little pack of well-worn prayer leaflets to saints like Padre Pio, St Therese and St Peregrine, as well as various novenas. Many others pray the Divine Mercy Devotion or the Cursillo prayers. Some people find it helpful just to repeat the name of 'Jesus' again and again. In an age where prayer is supposed to be obsolete, it is amazing how many people pray – many more than most people imagine. People pray in their own way, in ways with which they are comfortable.

In Derry City and the North West, there are many people who were born or have roots in the Donegal Gaeltacht. Even in old age, they still recite the prayers of their childhood in the language in which they originally learned them, *as Gaeilge*. They have some beautiful prayers that, I hope, are being handed on to coming generations.

In my ministry, I discreetly try to discover whether people are accustomed to prayer – and, if so, what kind of prayers they pray and how they pray. I try to meet them where they are at and pray with them in that situation. I see it as my role to adapt myself to a form of prayer that the patient is comfortable with, or to assist patients who have lost familiarity with prayer. Prayer should be uplifting and relaxing – it should ease people's fears – it should not make them uncomfortable or bored. It should induce peace and calm into people's hearts.

Many people who are aware that death is approaching tend to recall their childhood and the people who populated that part of their lives, especially their parents – they are inclined to recall people who have died many years ago – they love to recount experiences, happy and unhappy. I have travelled the oceans with men who served all their lives in the merchant navy. One gentleman, in particular, springs to mind. He passed the long and lonely hours away on voyages from oil terminals in the Persian Gulf to delivery points in all parts of the globe by teaching himself the melodeon and playing it! He seemed to spend every spare moment on it. He insisted on taking it with him when he was admitted to the Hospice. He did not play it very well; but he was happy and content. He also had a rosary – he told me that he had said the rosary every day – and the old well-fingered rosary and the well-used melodeon were his two companions during all those years on the high seas. Another patient had spent much of his life working on railways in Scotland. He loved talking about trains and railways, something in which I have to confess a personal interest! Shortly before he died, the hospice staff arranged a little surprise for him. Accompanied by a nurse, I took Robert to the Foyle Valley Railway Museum here in Derry and he was allowed, under supervision, to drive a railcar for about a mile or so along the railway line beside the river. Robert was utterly exhilarated with this experience. He died about two weeks later, but spent a lot of time during those last two weeks of his life talking about driving 'the train' along the banks of the Foyle. Women talk to me about working in the shirt factories, about bringing up their families in small, inadequate houses in hard times. Elderly people, themselves grandparents, love to talk about their parents. Every person has a story to tell. Most people love telling that story and having someone to listen to it.

Hospice care is about living, rather than dying. Patients often arrive with us haggard, emaciated and weary. In some situations, they have suffered severe hair loss because of their illness or treatment; in other cases, their hair is unkempt. Some are depressed and their self-esteem is low. The hospice staff endeavour to address those problems in various ways, not least by ensuring the patients' comfort. The beds are of a very high quality and so is the food. Jacuzzis are available and, in our Day Centre, there are various forms of therapy, reflexology, aromatherapy, hairdressing, art, music and everything in between. I think it is good, on occasion, to ask the family to bring in a photograph of the patient portraying the way he or she looked in happier and healthier times. The photograph is then placed in a prominent position in the room, where it serves as a conversation topic and gives staff an idea of how the patient looked at a time when he or she was in better health; this helps them to see beyond the mask of sickness. Amazingly, this little gesture does wonders for the patient's self-esteem. We endeavour to make the patient as comfortable as possible and, above all, give them their dignity. The dignity of the patient is all important.

Again and again, I have witnessed the transformation that comes about when patients experience hospice care. Frightened individuals become tranquil and peaceful; they learn to smile again. People racked with pain become relatively pain-free, and the quality of life and relationships of both the patient and the patient's family and the interaction between them are enhanced to a remarkable degree.

There are occasions when this transformation does not take place, but these are rare.

CHAPTER 4

The Family

HOSPICE CARE involves care of the patient's family as well as care of the patient. From the moment a patient is admitted, we endeavour to get to know the family of the patient and offer them support. When someone who is loved receives a prognosis that indicates a terminal illness, it causes ripples of anguish and anxiety throughout the family circle. The intensity of the distress may vary according to the age of the patient, but, whatever the age, it is always a traumatic experience for everyone concerned.

In the Foyle Hospice there are various facilities for the families of patients. There are lounges or rooms where people may rest and relax. There is a kitchen where relatives can make a cup of tea or coffee or a light meal. We have three apartments, where relatives from out-of-town may be accommodated overnight. Each apartment consists of a bedroom, a small kitchen and a bathroom with a shower. This facility enables families of patients to stay at the hospice twenty-four hours a day when the patient is very ill.

The doctors and nurses are easily accessible for any family member who wishes to ask questions or discuss the patient's condition. I make myself available for counselling and prayer to relatives where that is requested or required. In my daily Communion round, I offer the Eucharist to family members where and when that is appropriate.

In the current environment where family breakdown is more prevalent, there can be many and various domestic situations that require considerable sensitivity. The best and most effective lessons are learned from situations where one behaved stupidly or insensitively. One such occasion occurred when I entered a room the day after a male patient was admitted. A woman and young girl about ten years old were in the room. I recognised the young girl, because she had been in the room the previous evening – she was the patient's daughter. I had not met the woman before and did not recognise her. Breezily, I said to the young girl, 'Is this your Mum?', and she casually replied, 'No, Joan is Daddy's girl friend!'[2] There followed a long moment of embarrassed silence on the part of all concerned. I never asked such a question again in similar circumstances!

In a situation where death is imminent, people are often extremely fraught and fragile. Grief and anxiety give rise to fragility. The patient may raise issues about relationships. Sometimes members of the family raise these issues. Many people

---

2   Joan is not her real name

experience fractures in the family. It is perhaps a result of the pressure of modern living. A family member, son or daughter, has broken contact with the family – perhaps gone abroad and just lost contact; or developed problems of one kind or another and contact was deliberately broken off. As death approaches, the patient frequently asks to see such people. They are anxious to make contact again before death intervenes. If I am asked to help, in such circumstances, before doing anything, I will usually discuss the matter with other members of the family and seek to learn what they think about the proposal. In almost every incidence of this, the reunion was achieved, usually with copious tears being shed on all sides. A great healing took place and a sense of peace was generated in both the patient and other members of family and, of course, the 'stranger' as well. I have come, in recent years, to a new understanding and insight into the parable of the prodigal son. It is not just the heavenly father or mother who misses such a person – the earthly parent misses them too. 'While he was still a long way off, his father saw him and was moved with pity. He ran to the boy, clasped him in his arms and kissed him tenderly'. (Luke 15:20). All of life is truly in the Gospels.

Some other problems are much more complex and difficult to resolve in such a satisfactory manner. Whilst most couples have wonderful, loving marriages, other couples are not so fortunate. In some cases, the patient has entered a second relationship. Often, there are children from both relationships. When a request is made to facilitate a short meeting with the former partner, it requires delicate and sensitive handling. In some cases, the request comes from the former partner, sometimes from the patient. Each situation is different. The request is always taken seriously. The various children of the relationships have to be taken into consideration. Sometimes, the absent spouse or partner is unwilling and uninterested, fearful of the hurt that possibly could be involved. In some cases, with great generosity on all sides, it is possible to facilitate such requests. In other situations, it is clear that it will only serve to make an already difficult situation much worse. I try to remain neutral in such circumstances. Whilst I have gladly facilitated such meetings, I have never initiated them. The initiative comes either from the patient, members of the patient's family or from the former spouse or partner. It is certainly a good and wonderful experience when it can take place, but it can be very difficult and needs to be handled with great delicacy.

In-patients are with us for various periods – sometimes only for a few days – sometimes for a few months. If the patient is with us for a few weeks or months, there is an opportunity to come to know the family and friends very well. During visits, especially in the evening, I would take the opportunity to spend a short time in prayer with the patient and his or her visitors – perhaps recite some evening or night prayers together or read a psalm or passage from the New Testament. The hospice has many nooks and quiet areas where relatives sit and rest where there is an opportunity to chat and discuss things with them. I have a little room that serves as my office and it is also a place where I do some counselling if and when that is requested or necessary.

Family members come from all over the world to watch and wait at the bedside of a parent or loved one. One elderly patient had three adult children – her daughter was in Hong Kong, and her two sons were in New Zealand and Canada. At all times, one of them was at her bedside and, during the last week of her life, all three of them were there. For some families, it is the first occasion when they are all, as adults, thrown closely together for a protracted period of time. It can be a very special time for a family – a time of reminiscing and bonding – a time for recalling experiences of childhood and expressing love and appreciation to parents and to one another. Recently, we had a middle-aged patient who was one of a family of eighteen. His mother, Kathleen, a wonderful woman, is still alive and well and was present at his bedside, with other members of the family, during his illness. It was edifying to observe the love of that woman for her family and the faith that radiated from her. This was reflected by the family in their love and care for her. The recitation of the Rosary around that bed with that family was particularly memorable and edifying.

When and where possible, I try to encourage each family member to seek out some time alone with the patient, and to take the opportunity to thank them, to express their appreciation and, if necessary, to seek their forgiveness. It can be a difficult and emotional experience. Patient and visitor both greatly appreciate such opportunities. So many of us have had the experience of a parent dying suddenly and unexpectedly and we never had an opportunity to say our goodbyes. It is good to have such an opportunity and to avail of it.

We have had a number of parents of young children as patients over the years. There are particular issues to be addressed when there are young children involved. Each case has to be taken individually. Some patients, especially mothers, are concerned about how their children will react to their appearance, with all the medical accoutrements, drips and lines and so on. The views of the healthy parent must be carefully respected in matters like these. The medical staff will offer guidance in such situations. I tend to think that it is better when young children are permitted to visit the terminally ill parent as frequently as is feasible. Whether and when they should be told the full extent and inevitable consequence of the parent's illness are other matters that require discussion. The age and temperament of the child have to be taken into consideration. Children can often surprise. I clearly remember one ten-year-old girl, not long after I began my service as chaplain, who insisted on taking one of the readings at Mass all during her mother's time in the Hospice. She read clearly and intelligently, without any nervousness or inhibition and showed remarkable courage and understanding of the situation. She was fully aware of the situation. She was a great support to her father and her mother was so proud of her. Some young children have the capacity of understanding and coping with the situation extraordinarily well. In years gone by, young children were often shipped off to an aunt or uncle when a parent became terminally ill; sometimes, they did not return until after the funeral. It was the culture of the time. I do not think that that was satisfactory. I am sure that it bred resentment in future years; understandable resentment, perhaps, that one was ignored or deprived and not made privy to the full truth about a parent's condition. The final decision on such matters, however, must be decided by the parent who is the patient and the patient's spouse. Whilst all kinds of advice may be given, it is their decision and theirs alone. That decision should be respected.

Teenage children can often present much greater difficulty than younger children in these circumstances. Some of them tend to clam up; they do not even want to discuss the situation or talk about it. Some do not want even to go the bedside of their ailing parent. They try to put on a brave and strong face, whilst, in fact, they feel insecure, frustrated and angry. Death is simply not on their agenda. They do not want to think of it. Tender caring attention and gentle support needs to be given to young people in such situations.

The families of our patients give great support to one another. During their time in the hospice, each family gets to know the other families and they become very effective support groups for each other. We have a kitchen where relatives can make tea or coffee or prepare light meals. This room is a meeting place for everyone. People talk about all kinds of things as well as topics of mutual concern. They share their worries and celebrate their little victories when their patient has had a better day than anticipated. There is another room which is an all too popular meeting place as well – the smoking room – I jokingly call it 'the marijuana room'! It is the only place in the hospice where smoking is permitted and is, without doubt, the most uncomfortable and unattractive room in the building. Patients and members of families who smoke go there to indulge in their habit. I was a cigarette smoker for more than thirty years – I gave up smoking more than twenty years ago. However, I simply cannot understand how anyone who witnesses at first hand the devastation that cigarette smoking causes can continue to smoke. We witness the most graphic evidence of that devastation in the hospice every day. But, despite witnessing such things, some people continue to smoke. The addiction to tobacco or nicotine is as powerful as it is life-threatening.

The families of our patients are a very important component of the hospice family. They play a very important part in the day to day life of the hospice. I have witnessed many family members grow and mature in these circumstances; younger members taking more responsibility; family bonds becoming closer. After their experience in the hospice many family members promote the hospice and seek support for it in various ways.

Now and again, we have a patient who is the last of a line – who emigrated, worked abroad or served in the merchant navy or in the forces – and never got married. He may not have any family surviving here – but still wishes to come home to die in the area where he has his roots. Such patients, and they are usually men, are not lacking in friendship here. There are people who come to visit and who care for him and ensure that he needs for nothing.

CHAPTER 5

Sunday Mass in the Hospice

MASS IS CELEBRATED in the hospice each Sunday morning. We have two ecumenical services each year. Chaplains and clergy from the other denominations come and celebrate Holy Communion or other services with their patients, as they feel necessary.

We have a small ecumenical chapel and it is the location for our Sunday Mass. This chapel opens out on to a large reception area. The Catholic patients and members of their families gather in the chapel. Members of staff and other people assemble in the reception area and assist in the Mass. Between sixty and one hundred people assist at Mass in the hospice each Sunday morning.

There is never a time when the sense of the hospice family is more present and vibrant than at the Sunday Mass. All the constituents of the hospice family are there, all are involved – the patients, their families, the hospice staff and families of former patients, praying with one another and for one another as a worshipping community. Each patient who is able to be present at Mass is individually greeted and mentioned by name. We also name and pray for all the other patients in the hospice on that particular morning. Each Sunday, those who have died during the previous week are remembered and their family members are welcomed. This practice has been created as a result of suggestions down through the years by people who join in the celebration. I was nervous and hesitant initially about publicly mentioning those who had died in the previous week, but after consultation with staff members, patients and families, it was determined that they should be mentioned individually. We mark anniversaries of patients who died at that time in previous years and their family members often attend. Family members of recently deceased patients usually attend our Mass for a few weeks after their bereavement, before returning to their own worshipping parish community. We have a fine choir and some readers and a small core of people who come to our Mass every Sunday and look after the Liturgy. These people give generously of their time and skills. People of all faiths are made welcome and attend from time to time.

We celebrate the Mass and Liturgy of the Sunday, but there is a keen awareness of the location and circumstances of the celebration. There is the consciousness of the Supper Room about it. I am always very aware of the words of Jesus in the Supper Room. In the very first words of chapter sixteen of St John's Gospel Jesus said 'I have

told you all this that your faith may not be shaken'
(John 16:1). Mass in the hospice is always a
celebration and the participation is wonderful. It is
challenging to preach in such a situation. I usually
allow the scriptural readings of the day or the
theme of the season to determine the subject or
theme of my homily. At the Last Supper, Jesus was
very conscious of what lay ahead and he wished to
give courage to his disciples; he told them not to be
afraid. He gave them the wonderful gift of the
Eucharist to sustain them. The imminent death of
someone you love, especially when that someone is
relatively young, can shake one's faith to the core
and test it. In St John's Gospel, Jesus goes on to
speak about his impending death and seeks to
reassure the disciples. 'I have told you all this so
that you may find peace in me. In the world you
will have trouble, but be brave: I have conquered
the world' (John 16:33).

In the Bidding Prayers, we try to embrace all the
different groups who are present. We pray for
patients asking that the Lord may support them,
sustain them, and help them to cope with their
illness. We ask for courage and for faith. We pray
for the families, thanking God for the love and
support that we find within the family, and ask for
strength and comfort. We pray for the doctors,
nurses, staff and volunteers who work in the
Hospice. We ask God to bless them for their
generosity and professionalism and their caring
skills. We pray for the dead, those who died during
the previous week, and those whose anniversaries

have occurred during the past week. We thank God for their lives and we pray that they be granted eternal rest. We are keenly conscious of the pain and loneliness that bereavement can bring. At every Mass in the Hospice, we greet the bereaved and pray that their suffering may be eased and that they will receive the blessing of comfort that Christ promised in the Beatitudes.

Mass in the hospice is a very personal and intimate liturgy – celebrated for a particular community with its own specific needs and fears and longings. Patients and family members always say that they are greatly comforted by their participation in it. I have been privileged to celebrate Mass in all kinds of places and situations for almost fifty years, but there is a very special atmosphere about the celebration of Mass in the hospice that I have never experienced in any other circumstances. There is a tangible feeling of community about it, a common sense of purpose, a group on pilgrimage together, very supportive of one another, very committed to one another, all of them acutely aware of what lies ahead or what has already occurred. My years in the hospice have brought me to a new appreciation of the priceless gift that we have in the Mass – the power of God's word and the wonder of the Eucharist.

CHAPTER 6

Last Days and Hours

IT IS A VERY special grace to be able to spend many of the last hours and days with a person who is nearing the end of his or her journey through this life. As the death of a loved one becomes imminent, friends and family wish to remain nearby. People watch at the bedside. They sit holding the patient's hand. They speak soft words gently to their friend. They embrace. There are long silences. Few words are spoken. Few words need to be spoken. When breathing becomes more difficult, there is a strange and powerful desire to help the person to breathe, to breathe with him or her – it is an extraordinary feeling that only those who have sat at the bedside of a dying friend know and have experienced. People come and go from the room. Some sob quietly. All are respectful. The nurses and doctors endeavour to make the patient as comfortable as possible.

It is a time for prayer – quiet and reflective prayer. There are suitable and beautiful readings in the *Pastoral Care of the Sick*. I already mentioned a particular passage from chapter fourteen in St

John's Gospel that has a special appeal to people who are very ill. They are words that have great significance during a vigil with someone who is dying. Let me quote the passage in full:

Jesus says:

'Do not let your hearts be troubled. Trust in God still, and trust in me. There are many rooms in my Father's house; if there were not, I should have told you. I am going now to prepare a place for you, and after I have gone and prepared you a place, I shall return to take you with me; so that where I am you may be too. You know the way to the place where I am going.'

Thomas said, 'Lord, we do not know where you are going, so how can we know the way?'

Jesus said: 'I am the Way, the Truth and the Life. No one can come to the Father except through me.

If anyone loves me he will keep my word, and my Father will love him, and we shall come to him and make our home with him.

Peace I bequeath to you, my own peace I give you, a peace the world cannot give, this is my gift to you. Do not let your hearts be troubled or afraid.' (*John* 14: 1-6, 23, 27)

At such times, I often read this passage quietly and slowly. It is full of comfort and reassurance. There are so many beautiful readings from scripture that can be used. There is nowhere that the true significance and value of the scriptures can be realised more profoundly than in situations of this nature. The Rosary is recited from time to time – members of the family each leading a decade. The prayer for a happy death, 'Jesus Mary and Joseph'[3] is recited. Each morning, in such circumstances, I conduct a short Eucharistic liturgy, with reading and prayers in the room. Those who wish to receive Holy Communion may do so. Public prayer should never be over-intrusive in these circumstances. Most of the time is best spent in silence. Prayer aloud should only serve to enrich the silence, the listening and watching, not to detract from it. Each individual is alone with his or her own thoughts. Each person watches every minute change in the patient's face or countenance, listens to the breathing.

It is interesting to observe the reactions of people to prayer at this stage. Some are awkward at first. It is obvious that they have not been all that familiar with prayer over the years. After a short time, in many cases, the awkwardness and unfamiliarity disappear. It is a prayer of faith reluctantly giving their loved one back to God and expressing gratitude and appreciation for all that they did.

Outside the room, people gather in little groups and chat quietly. Mobile phones ring with enquiries from friends. Other problems are left to one side.

---

3   For full prayer, see p 58

The world outside seems to have come to a standstill. At times like these, many people want to talk – to talk seriously about important, fundamental things. They frequently ask difficult and testing questions.

The doctors and members of the nursing staff will regularly meet with family members and update them on the patient's condition and of the treatment being administered. They will also respond to any concerns that family members may have.

When the dying process is protracted, as it sometimes is, going on for days and days, and perhaps into weeks, the question of euthanasia occasionally arises. In my experience, this question has never been raised by a patient, but it has been raised by family members on a few occasions – usually when they were extremely fatigued or anguished. On a couple of occasions, the family member implied or stated that this discussion was initiated by the patient. It is agonisingly difficult and painful to sit and watch life slowly ebb away from someone you dearly love. I should emphasise that these were all queries about euthanasia, rather than demands for euthanasia. Euthanasia has been in the news in recent times. I have no difficulty in understanding why such enquiries are made or such questions are asked. The reasons are perfectly understandable.

The Catholic Church teaching is clear 'Whatever its motives and means, direct euthanasia consists in putting an end to the lives of the handicapped, sick or dying persons. It is morally unacceptable'.[4] I believe that palliative care addresses this issue and gives due concern for patients and relatives. There may be the sincere and heartfelt appeal 'Please let my father die; let him get away; he has been through enough'. I believe that the skilled application of palliative care responds to that plea in a humane, morally and legally correct manner. A person can be helped to die, without killing them – dying can be made as easy as is humanly, morally and medically possible. The relevant passage in the Catechism is 'Even if death is thought imminent, the ordinary care owed to a sick person cannot be legitimately interrupted. The use of painkillers to alleviate the sufferings of the dying, even at the risk of shortening their days, can be morally in conformity with human dignity if death is not willed as either an end or a means, but only foreseen and tolerated as inevitable. Palliative care is a special form of disinterested charity. As such it should be encouraged'.[5] Arthur Hugh Clough, the English poet, in the mid-nineteenth century put it succinctly 'Thou shalt not kill: but need'st not strive officiously to keep alive'. The late Cardinal Franz König of Vienna said on one occasion 'People should be able to hold someone's hand when they are dying, but a human hand must never be the cause of their death'.[6]

---

4   *Catechism of the Catholic Church* (2277) Veritas Publications 1994
5   ibid., (2279)
6   Quoted in the homily at his funeral, March 2004

Palliative care, the form of medical care that keep patients pain-free is, I believe, the proper way to address this issue. As a lay person, I have observed the application of palliative care to terminally ill patients for the last ten years, and I have been always deeply impressed by the careful and conscientious manner in which it is administered and meticulously recorded by the medical staff. It is always administered under strict criteria. The dignity of the patient is paramount. As a result, everything humanly and morally possible is done to ensure that no hospice patient dies in great pain or distress.

CHAPTER 7

Death

The end came very quietly. I had left the room to make a phone call while my youngest brother and my sister were walking in the corridor, talking a little between the times they spent at mother's bedside. My father and younger brother sat on either side of mother's bed, following her breathing. It had become very quiet. The nurses had just rearranged the bed, washed mother's hands and face and combed her hair. All had become very quiet.

It was six o'clock in the evening. Father looked at her with full attention expecting that she might live for many hours. But then he noticed a definite slowing down of her breathing, saw her neck muscle make two more movements and realized that she had stopped breathing. Then he said to my brother 'She has died; call your brothers and sister'. As we stood around her bed we prayed the same prayers we had said so often during the past few days. But now I added for the first time the words we would say in the long days to come 'Eternal rest grant to her O Lord'.

She had simply stopped breathing. That was all. With carefully chosen words father told us about the final seconds of her life, how the end had come with a slight quiver of her neck 'It was hardly noticeable', he said, with a soft smile in his eyes. It had been so undramatic, so quiet. It had hardly been an event. For a moment, I felt sad because I had not been in the room. But then I realized that I should be grateful that father and mother had been so close on those last moments, I recognised that it was a gift that he, not I, could tell the story.[7]

The late Father Henri Nouwen thus described the death of his mother. The death of someone we love, and especially a parent, is something we never forget. It is a moment frozen in time, treasured in memory. We remember every detail, every little gesture, and every word spoken. We can remember precisely where we were and what we were doing.

No matter how often one witnesses a person dying, it is always an awesome moment. No two deaths are the same. A human life ends. It is the end of a story, the end of a journey, the end of a pilgrimage. A death in the hospice is usually a quiet

---

7   Henri JM Nouwen *In Memoriam* (Ave Maria Press, Notre Dame, Indiana 1980)

event – on occasions, it comes unexpectedly – in most cases, members of the family and close friends are gathered at the bedside, holding the hands of the patient – speaking to him or her, whispering, gently kissing or embracing the patient, sometimes sobbing quietly. Nobody likes to die alone. It is something many patients mention – they do not want to be alone when death comes.

We pray the prayer for a happy death and sprinkle holy water recalling the baptism that all of us share. Two candles are lit, reminding us of the light that is Jesus Christ. When Jesus spoke to the people again, he said: 'I am the light of the world; anyone who follows me will not be walking in the dark; he will have the light of life.' (*John* 8:12)

> Jesus Mary and Joseph, I give you my heart and soul
>
> Jesus Mary and Joseph assist me in my last agony
>
> Jesus Mary and Joseph, may I breathe forth my soul in peace with you,
> Amen
>
> Into your hands, O Lord, I commit my spirit Lord Jesus, receive my soul.
>
> O Sacred Heart of Jesus, I place all my trust in thee.

When the moment of death seems near, the Prayer of Commendation is recited:

I commend you, my dear brother/sister, to
almighty God,
and entrust you to your Creator.
May you return to him
who formed you from the dust of the earth.
May holy Mary, the angels and all the saints
come to meet you as go forth from this life.
May Christ who was crucified for you
bring you freedom and peace.
May Christ who died for you
admit you into his garden of paradise.
May Christ, the true Shepherd,
acknowledge you as one of his flock.
May he forgive all you sins,
and set you among those he has chosen.
May you see your Redeemer face to face
and enjoy the vision of God forever.
Amen.[8]

Some members of the nursing staff join the family
in the room. They bring a calm and peace to the
situation. They regularly ensure that the patient is
comfortable. Everyone listens to the breathing.
The breathing gradually becomes more laboured –
the time span between breaths significantly
increases. And then the breathing stops. There is
no great dramatic moment or memorable dying
words. It is all very quiet. Tears flow. People sob
and embrace. They comfort one another. It is a
very special moment that everyone present will

---

8   *Pastoral Care of the Sick* p 179

remember and recall in great detail in the days to come.

People usually like to remain in the room for some time after the death. Some families decide that each member of the family should have a little while alone at the bedside. Members of the hospice staff usually provide tea or coffee for the family in the reception area and after this I usually conduct a short prayer service for the family at the bedside.

> Eternal rest grant unto him/her, O Lord
> And let perpetual light shine upon him/her
> May he/she rest in peace
> Amen.

A death in the hospice has an impact on the other patients and families who happen to be there at that time. The Foyle Hospice is a relatively small unit, and, inevitably, the news of a death quickly spreads. Family members of all the patients meet one another frequently in the various rooms where relatives gather. Patients come to know one another through attendance at the Day Centre or attendance at Sunday Mass. If I think it is appropriate, I will advise other patients and their relatives of the death and we will pray together for the deceased and for the family of the deceased. Prayer, on such occasions, sometimes generates discussion about the patient's own death. On other occasions, there is no comment.

CHAPTER 8

Farewell

THE HOSPICE STAFF bids farewell at a short and simple service before the patient's remains are taken home. The patient's chaplain conducts this short service in the mortuary chapel. The service is attended by the family and friends of the deceased and some of the nurses and a doctor from the staff.

Out of the depths I cry to you, O Lord
Lord, hear my voice
O let your ears be attentive
to the voice of my pleading.

My soul is waiting for the Lord
I count on his word.
My soul is longing for the Lord
More than watchman for daybreak.

Because with the Lord there is mercy
And fullness of redemption,
Israel he will redeem
From all its iniquity.
(Psalm 129)

Afterwards the coffin with the remains of the deceased is carried to a hearse and we accompany the funeral procession for a short distance.

Here in the North West, the tradition of the wake in the home of deceased is still very strong. Burials usually take place about two days after death. In the interval between the death and the church service or Requiem Mass, the wake takes place. I believe that this is a good and healthy tradition. It is a very powerful and traditional form of grief therapy and is a cherished community tradition. Wakes and funerals are very well attended. In almost fifty years of priesthood, I have never come across drunkenness or other excesses at wakes. Like everyone else, I have read stories about these events, but I have never had any personal experience of this. I doubt very much that it was a widespread phenomenon. The wake gives the bereaved an opportunity to talk over and over again about the person who has died, about their life and death. It gives friends and neighbours an opportunity to express sympathy and appreciation. It is an opportunity for prayer. It is an occasion for neighbours to rally round the bereaved family – as well as emotional support, people bring loaves of sandwiches and other items to the wake house. Neighbours show great kindness and care on such occasions.

I was not aware until recently, that this tradition has disappeared in many parts of Ireland. I believe that the wake in the family home is a good and healthy tradition and serves a useful community purpose. It is also a prayerful occasion. I suspect that some psychological think tank in California in years to come will 'invent' the wake as a most effective form of bereavement therapy.

I mentioned already that many families attend Sunday Mass in the hospice in the weeks after the death of a family member. Many also come on the occasions of anniversaries, at Christmas or at times when they are feeling 'a little down' or lonely. The attachment to the hospice remains.

The hospice hosts a Support Group for the Bereaved. Bereaved people are invited to attend and to participate in the group. Two of our nurses facilitate this group along with some other people who have been through the experience of bereavement. The group is inter-denominational. People avail of this service when or where it is felt necessary. The course consists of weekly meetings for six weeks. People are free to attend one or more of these courses. It is much appreciated and does excellent work.

People in the North West now wonder how they managed before the Foyle Hospice came into being. It is difficult to believe that it has only been there since 1991. During that time, more than 1,100 patients have been treated there. I hope that hospices will soon be established in more communities and provide the specialised comforts and care that they are uniquely qualified to deliver to people who are terminally ill, and to their families. I also hope that governments and health boards will decide to give hospices an adequate level of grant aid and support.

I remember sitting with a patient one lovely autumn evening a few years ago. It was just getting dark. We had prayed together and we were both sitting and looking out the window at the lights of the traffic busily moving to and fro on the Foyle Bridge. She had told me earlier about how peaceful and happy she was. Then she smiled and quietly said to me 'This is like God's waiting room'.

Recommended Reading

Sheila Cassidy, *Sharing the Darkness*, London: Darton Longman & Todd, 1988

Michael Kearney, *Mortally Wounded*, Dublin: Mercier Press, 1996

Andrew McGrady, Ed., *Come Lord Jesus – Prayers for the Time of Dying*, Dublin: Veritas, 1992

Henri J.M. Nouwen, *In Memoriam*, Notre Dame, Indiana: Ave Maria Press, 1980